Damned Welcome:

Aesthetic Realism Maxims

The unknown is coming 'round the block.

DAMNED WELCOME
Aesthetic Realism Maxims

By Eli Siegel

SECOND EDITION

Drawings by Chaim Koppelman

DEFINITION PRESS   NEW YORK   1972

Damned Welcome was first published by the Terrain Gallery
and is reprinted by arrangement.

Library of Congress Catalog Card Number 71-171394

Standard Book Number (hard cover edition) 910492-17-4
Standard Book Number (paperback edition) 910492-18-2

Printed in the United States of America

CONTENTS

ILLUSTRATIONS

PREFACE

Why do people have mental trouble? Aesthetic Realism says, Because they don't like the world enough. In maxim form this would be: Avoid trouble with yourself by liking the world more. This is a sober and short statement put in rather plain English; and I think it is true in Madagascar and Montmartre, in 50 B.C. and at just this moment. The question is, though, How to like the world? Another question is, What does it mean to like the world?

The first thing necessary for liking the world is to be interested in knowing what the world is, and what it is about. It is surprising, saddening, almost stupefying to see the lack of desire, known and unknown, to know what the world wholly and truly is about. Many persons have thought: It isn't necessary to know the world;

*what is necessary is to do a convenient or com-
fortable job with the part of it you just have to
meet. And Aesthetic Realism says, You can't do
a comfortable job with the world unless you
want to know it.*

*In previous Aesthetic Realism publications,
the meaning of liking-and-knowing the world for
one's own good has been considered in quite a
few careful paragraphs. In this publication, liking-and-knowing the world is presented in all
kinds of swift sentences. There are three good
reasons for appreciating the universe, or the great
Everything Besides Oneself. One, the universe
deserves to be appreciated; two, it is bad for a
person if he doesn't appreciate the universe: he
feels guilty, is in conflict, acts confusedly, etc.;
three, a good and wonderful and comely time
can be had in studying how to appreciate the
tremendously puzzling and yet benign universe.*

*These maxims are, then, in behalf of a world
too often seen as unkind, dull, and just too
bewildering for anything. It is better to be be-
wildered by an Aesthetic Realism Maxim about*

things than by things themselves.   The universe can speak for itself, but, as everyone knows, it is so easy for it to go unheard, because of the uncouthness of its language, and the seeming bad news it has so often to tell.   We should all of us assist in presenting the message of the stones, of history, of motion, of forms, of time, of death, of hands, of selves, of thistles, and of rocks. Their message is the message of what's real.

So far, most maxims have had a sad or cynical ring.   Some lovely maxims have seemed withering.   The present maxims, however they may seem, are on the side of a reasoned gaiety, and a spontaneous, bubbling seriousness.   They are meant to bother into appreciation.   Their purpose is to sustain by leaps.

—ELI SIEGEL

PART ONE

1
Don't shake the hand of reality with one finger.

2
Psychiatrists are too much like most people and not enough like most people: in both cases it's unfortunate.

3
Parings from your fingernails have gone to where you came from.

4
A dewdrop has good news to tell which lasts after it is gone.

5
Why we do something should be charming.

6
If our theory is better than our practice, it's because it and we haven't grown up.

7
A person who thinks he doesn't like people, and yet is nice to them, has theory not caught up with practice: this occurs often.

8
In the unconscious generally, there are many instances of theory which has not caught up with practice.

9
If you tap nervously with your fingers on a piano, you make a piano an accomplice to something.

10
Lettuce is looking for its best year next year.

11
The dirt between one's toes didn't get there just by wishing.

12
Hope is a red petal wanting to know what the fire's about.

13
A doorknob turns around on itself, but doesn't have its own way.

*All the leaps into the air, thought of together,
leave room for more.*

14

A key at the bottom of the ocean and a key on a desert can meet in your own mind, and that way attain new usefulness.

15

Smoking a cigarette, you can, without condescension, think of people who never did.

16

All the leaps into the air, thought of together, leave room for more.

17

Dancing shows space is useful.

18

The seat of a chair of 1676 *can,* if you think hard enough, make you a little less tired.

19

The cheerful rat-tat-tat of a drum is a defiance of thin, cruel lips.

20

Divinity can be lush.

21

The snapping of suspenders has its place in trans-Mississippi history.

22
People who crossed oceans, years ago, have mostly stopped doing so; this is not cause for unmixed regret.

23
A flute has a message to be distinguished from that of a bassoon.

24
The weight of all eyelashes is overpowering.

25
It was arranged that a mouse be timid, that we should say so, and that timidity be disapproved.

26
We should think of a hippopotamus in terms of its milieu; yet to think of a hippopotamus in other than its milieu helps.

27
An orchestra can be a benevolent, conspiratorial aggregate.

28
Two people, meeting suddenly, can suddenly find it was worth while; then again, it may take longer.

29

Holding a diamond between your fingers, or a page of a great, lovely folio, should make you look on your finger joints with new zeal and respect.

30

You can write in any language on your calf.

31

Our loveliest memories can be helped by our most fundamental hopes.

32

Criticism always asks, "What is the hesitation for?" and always says, "Get in there and fight"; it really can't do otherwise.

33

An assumption, as such, is really not more daring than the facts.

34

Sighs should be efficient; if not, we should long for their departure.

35

Everything should say: I remind you.

36
A storm has a plan you don't get at first notice.

37
If you do something else, it should be just as good.

38
The aroma of an onion is in friendly competition with that of mignonette; if you look hard, you can't distinguish the competition from partnership.

39
Ask more of yourself and you'll find there are stocks on hand; or a new shipment hovering around.

40
Time can be cracked by thought.

41
Your wrists are one of your best friends.

42
X   If you have time, remember it's a privilege.

43
X   Respect for anything is an achievement not a donation: if you respect space it is a victory for

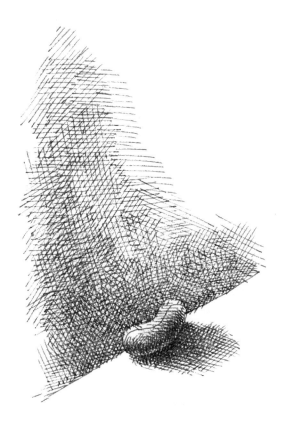

The tremendousness of the word it *can be seen in that* it *(the word) can stand for infinity and a bean and the combination of infinity and a bean: we should emulate this respectable pronoun.*

you; and if you find more to respect in an uncle or in a businessman in America of the 1840s, a desire of yours has been attained, and discreetly you may congratulate yourself.

44
The tremendousness of the word *it* can be seen in that *it* (the word) can stand for infinity and a bean and the combination of infinity and a bean: we should emulate this respectable pronoun.

45
You is the word *I* enlarged; *he* is the result of the enlarging process continued.

46
A certain novel wasn't written in the eighteenth century; its absence wasn't complained of: this shows the restraint possible in centuries.

47
We should forgive that which we won't have to forgive ourselves for forgiving.

48
Time and space have such ease.

49
Events rebuke us, and we shouldn't mind.

50
The planets show grandeur and nicety in their operations; the question is, how did they learn this?

51
Both poetry and sex should have delicacy-and-a-tiger.

52
When we are happy we should have a definite sense of being for the Great Lakes, et cetera; nothing less will do.

53
All "these things" were once "those things."

54
No kitchen matches, I suppose, are in the planet Saturn: this matter should not end here.

55
Every period in history is current.

56
A pessimist is a person who finds an oyster in a pearl.

57
His mother seemed annoyed to the little Assyrian

child, and he never found out whether she was or not.

58
X When you care for something truly, pat yourself on the back.

59
X Love should be seen as a restriction on our incompleteness.

60
X Love is a way of giving another person her way in a manner useful to us.

61
X All love is first love.

62
What Napoleon did it for, is a tremendous case history.

63
The Elizabethans shouldn't be considerably more interested in Elizabethans than we are.

64
X An ocean is a decision of infinity.

65
A nation consists of people who may think now and then that they're a nation.

66
Geography is a way things have of doing things.

67
A memory of an event can creep up closer and closer.

68
X The victory of birth shouldn't be changed into a drawn battle.

69
X The universe is Why, How, and What, in any order, and all at once.

70
The weight of the universe is at one with all its space.

71
The universe, being clever, has given scientists trouble.

72
X Art is a way of showing greater fairness to things than is customary.

73
How did a universe, if unfair, make man desire fairness and object to unfairness?

74
We can say Here in 752, and There in this very year; Here in Nineveh, and There in Scranton.

75
The wonderful dogs us.

76
People need people to be new people.

77
A man needs everything he can lay his mind on.

78
A world complained of expects you to do something about it; it has furnished you the complaint, and can furnish you the means of dealing with it.

79
If the world is rude, it is looking to man to teach it not to be.

80
Man and the world are the world; Ruth and America are America.

81
A thing is everything the rest of the world isn't.

82
The fates like bold, graceful answers and happy questions.

83
If the world has dealt with you badly personally, it has at least taken a lot of trouble.

84
When a ghost talks critically of you, talk back.

85
When your conscience accuses you, take down the main points.

86
The unconscious is always giving advice.

87
You learn something from anything by thinking about it.

88
Everything is up to something, and everything doesn't mind if you know what it is.

89
The ornamental wants justice done to it.

90
Ecstasy is a way of knowing a few answers.

91
To love more is to love with sincerity.

92
When remorse is proper and triumph is improper, much can be said for remorse.

93
Braggadocio and tears show the versatility of the human conscience.

94
Coffee, drunk, meets the ego, the self, et cetera.

95
The Missouri River is still taking its time; some aspects of Niagara Falls have been in a hurry for centuries.

96
When people are not themselves, they are not wholly something else, either.

97
X   Girls in novels do things to girls not in novels.

98
X   The room for improvement we have should be comfortable.

99
That sweet girl who lived next door lived in the same period of history as he did.

100
Hummingbirds lived before and after machinery.

101
A girl with large aims can wash socks better because she has them.

102
One sign of being intellectual is to think that intellect and potatoes have something in common.

103
The world went after mountain tops, and got them.

104
It is sufficient to be not against perfection.

One sign of being intellectual is to think that intellect and potatoes have something in common.

105
The way the clock did not fall from the mantelpiece was perfect.

106
Her better self was a poor relative much too often.

107
People have died not knowing where they disagreed with themselves.

108
Substance is what a thing can't do without; form is what a thing can't be without; mind is what a thing can't live without.

109
If you say the truth, so much you follow the truth; and truth follows you; and you reach the truth and the truth reaches you; and there's a quiet and definite little celebration at this time which many people don't know about.

110
The idea, of course, is just as much a part of a human being as his epiglottis.

111

The bad mystic becomes the All by diminishing it.

112

Vanity, being so much like pride, has been hard to distinguish, and so it has been called 2-A by Aesthetic Realism; and this 2-A will grow either stronger or weaker with each new thing in one's life.

113

The self will go to any limit to be what it wants; ego will accept any limit to be comfortable.

114

We are original when we can see originality in others.

115

The world consists of things and other things happening to things.

116

Whatever invented fingernails is still around.

117

Big toes speak to hair follicles.

118
X   When we don't think right and our heart beats right, the heart has opposition.

119
If we had the time we could give each blood cell an alluring name.

120
Dust can come to books in which the Sun God, Apollo, is described.

121
X   A ship is a certain way of bringing out the possibilities of waves.

122
Foam and froth can be thought of for an hour at a time.

123
A battle-axe can not be used for 8,000 years.

124
X   Nausea can be unclearly accepted self-condemnation.

125
A moth will be a moth until.

126
A sensible person living on earth discriminates among an infinite field.

127
The fact that stormy weather can be described in measured prose should give one hope.

128
You can find aesthetics in underbrush with no flattery to the underbrush.

129
We should see the American Revolution in proportion to our own distress.

130
We should be able to greet any 4 A.M. with applause.

131
An electric fan whirring near a newly mowed lawn, can be thought of by itself.

132
X
Energy, like grammar, should be used correctly; the unjust expenditure of energy or its unjust withholding should cease immediately.

133
✗ The tearful things the wind has to tell should be better understood.

134
Ice is a way water has of telling you, you shouldn't make up your mind about it too quick.

135
Either a hummingbird or a rabbit may be ahead in a meadow.

136
✗ Every really correct notion of a bad thing is charming.

137
Poems have mystery, languor, and point.

138
✗ We all have in us the makings of ourselves.

139
✗ If a mistake is not a stepping stone, it is a mistake.

140
✗ It is also important to find out what we haven't been talking about.

141
X
When you have the steadiness of an ocean and the touch of a pickpocket (without the intention), you can deal with people better.

142
X
Every work of art is about everything.

143
Everything is acting and waiting to act.

144
X
The years of the past are taking it easy; but are looking for developments.

145
X
Our attitude towards concepts should be possessive.

146
X
To find something that in *no* way can make one happier is *so* difficult.

147
The frail and uncertain personality of Miss Starkweather was also cruel.

148
When the lovely both is looked for and astonishes, things are going as they should.

149

All persons you have met are in your mind, so you might as well arrange them properly.

150

We should not look on the planet Uranus from the point of view of an outsider.

151

We should change our minds because of our steadiness of true purpose.

152

Love is justice in a crisis.

153

Justice is versatile.

154

You can see a wrong thing rightly, and a right thing wrongly: this shows you can't tell what truth will do next.

155

That person must be beautiful who has an intense knowledge of beauty; those who don't think so have an insufficient equipment in the matter of loveliness.

156

X Our hopes should put the future into good shape.

157

X The purpose of regret is to avoid it.

158

X Love can grow no faster than the person loving.

159

Most celebrations of birthdays haven't covered the subject.

160

The things Aristotle, Hazel Neff, and Francis Bacon agree on might surprise all three.

161

Part of what the world has up its sleeve will be known by you tomorrow between 3 and 8 P.M.

162

The greater the imagination, the more moral it is.

163

X When an artist unconsciously doesn't like being an artist, and comes to feel bad, he shouldn't say it's because he's an artist.

164

X When nature makes both whales and bees, and makes them well, it isn't just showing off.

165

X The eyelashes of a man are still delicate while he stamps his foot.

166

The next moment should help a certain moment five days ago.

167

Logic can be whispered.

168

The way we are vexed ought to be improving constantly.

169

An onion skin can be contemplated for twenty minutes exactly.

170

X Sex ought to be a way of people's getting really together.

171

X When we honor rightly, we should be honored.

172

X

Real gratitude is a sign that we deserve something; and the deserving makes the gratitude pleasurable.

173

X –

A person is courageous who is comfortable in larger territory than is usual.

174

X

The nearer effort and desire are one, the better for them.

175

– X

We can now calmly consider future confusions.

176

There is no reason why a glass can't be broken in the twenty-first century, particularly under the right auspices.

177

A story could be written about how a table wasn't wiped, which could thrill no end: send the blood coursing swiftly through you.

178

The spaces between your fingers have a history of their own.

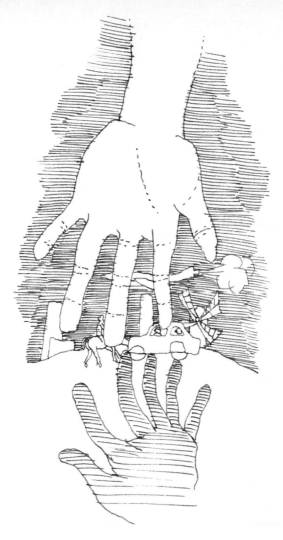

The spaces between your fingers have a history of their own.

179
Eighteen grass blades and eighteen men show a little what the number 18 can do.

180
The meaning of a rose petal won't end where your thoughts may.

181
When a thing is beautiful—a sentence, a cup, a smile, a fabric, a color, a chord, a dance—it is because the world as it deeply, truly is, got into it.

182
If you call Helen of Troy, A, and Cleopatra, B, you don't have to be wasting your time, particularly if you know how to go on from there.

183
Since a sour-faced, thin-minded spinster is born from erotic play, this shows the erotic does not tear down all barriers.

184
Technically perfect dactyls can be written of sudden nakedness.

185
When you are sad, you should be able to stand up for the reason.

186
A mind cannot be adjusted to a world which it makes less than it is, or accepts as less than it is; if a mind is not adjusted to infinity, maladjustment is around.

187
A concept is now looking for embodiment.

188
A neurotic is a person who rings doorbells hoping nobody is in.

189
A ghost is a person without any burdens—at least not the kind Grand Central Station recognizes.

190
A man is an animal who can move his hands while thinking of how he once moved his hands while thinking of something else.

191
A tree is something which shows the earth can go straight.

192
The sentence "I love you" is entirely grammatical.

The sentence "I love you" is entirely grammatical.

193
The world is in a constant state of love and rebellion as to what it was.

194
The self should be a tradition and a trumpet call.

195
Metaphysics gets around more than germs.

196
The poem to be written tomorrow likes its predecessors.

197
The year 2141 isn't as lonely as you think.

198
X You have consented to be what you are, and you may consent not to like it.

199
Poetry has in it onion skin, warehouses, and crags; and it's still looking around.

200
X A letter can be deep emotions on a smooth, white surface.

201
X
Love should be a way of giving the best in us to the person who can take it best.

202
Most plays have been missed.

203
The risk of seeing a bad play after having had a good meal should be thought about.

204
There were more elbows than people in ancient Britain.

205
Julius Caesar has been talked of nearly 37 times longer than he was talked to.

206
X
Unfortunately, millions of people walk around thinking ill of millions of people.

207
X
No person was lonely who was entirely against being lonely.

208
English tenses should remain long after the going of the British Empire.

The defeat of ego and prejudice by lucidity and energy makes the angels roll in the aisles.

209
Grief is bad in proportion as there is shame in it.

210
If you do the right thing, you do it for every-body.

211
Minds are in a great cooperative.

212
All the tears of the past have dried.

213
All the eyebrow-lifting in the world hasn't changed the value of anything.

214
A bore is a person who tries to interest you without having your interest at heart.

215
We can touch mid-Pacific with our fingertips.

216
Not understanding others is worse than not being understood by them.

217
The defeat of ego and prejudice by lucidity and energy makes the angels roll in the aisles.

218
Poetry shows that different two-and-twos can make different fours from what you expected.

219
X A ribbon tied around the earth would be deserved.

220
X Uncertainty has been expressed in all languages.

221
Two icebergs being looked at by three persons for two minutes can be thought of by one person.

222
For the last twenty minutes the Gulf Stream has been that.

223
X A clarinet falling downstairs shows it is like many other things.

224
X There is hope for all confusion.

225
English prose style has a future which makes demands on English prose style to describe.

226

Innocence arrived at is greater than innocence begun with.

227

A poor thing should not be let alone.

228

There is a relation among all the motives in the world like the relation among all colors and lines; this in a way means that all motives lead to the same thing.

229

If you like yourself for the wrong reason, you will dislike yourself for the right reason.

230

When we don't want people to get the hard facts about ourselves, we are not in favor of these three things: the facts, people, ourselves.

231

Rosebud lips, kissed under the blue sky, employ the sky for something.

232

All words have their origins: its origin is one of the reasons you may use one of these words tomorrow.

233
When a twig falls on a drum, this shows you can't think of twigs too restrictedly.

234
Mind shows the ambitions of matter.

235
Orange juice and the Parthenon can both be commented on coolly at 4:10 P.M.

236
Spelling the word *terrible* right shows what you can be right about.

237
A schizophrenic has broken a contract, made at birth, with the world.

238
Vapor, rising from a kettle, cannot go anywhere: yet it's free.

239
A bird flying over a strange city need not know that the city is strange for its wings to be tired.

240
Mind is undulating and rocky because it has to keep up with what it meets.

241
Soapsuds on a brute are still soft.

242
Hell is where dullness is unopposed.

243
A real passion is controlled, because there's no need to control it.

244
Geology is as impetuous as it can be; and history is as swift as it can be; and a great moment as slow as it can be.

245
Leaves, when they rustle, nod approval both to the tree and to the earth from which they come.

246
We should hasten for the same reason that notes rightly, at times, hasten in music.

247
A person with an ugly mind, and with his finger-nails well manicured, is both worse and better than you may take him to be.

248
The heart beats: "Thank you," "Allons," and "Let me see."

249
Ugliness in the American House of Representatives is akin to ugliness in a miniature.

250
X Real ecstasy helps the community.

251
X We can have a good feeling about a bad one.

252
All the bits of eggshell now in South Africa should not be contemplated unless with definite advantage.

253
A ladder in a dream can take as many words to describe as one not in a dream.

254
Oysters, wet dishrags, and hippopotami are only a hint of something; deserts, volcanoes, and dry bones in the sun are also only a hint.

255
X Originality in art puts charm where it wasn't.

256
What villainy there was in the fourth century A.D., should not be forgiven now.

Oysters, wet dishrags, and hippopotami are only a hint of something; deserts, volcanoes, and dry bones in the sun are also only a hint.

257
A child's whimper can be seen, and should be, from a psychological, biological, sociological, anthropological, and historical point of view.

258
Every object is politely and persistently looking for your accurate attention.

259
The dithers, whirls, and gyrations of the past can now be observed methodically.

260
Mediaeval love maintained its beauty when the Renaissance came along.

261
To hate a falsely ornate writer points to the true possibilities in hate.

262
The history of Austria should surprise more people.

263
The fact that Vienna is on the Danube is a hard one.

264
Life is in, say, 8,000 parts of our body.

265
The ugliness and mediocrity in the streets of ancient Alexandria have vanished in the healing mists of time—if you prefer, they haven't.

266
Quintus Calpurnius was bored in the year 146 B.C.; he frantically gasped for breath in the year 142 B.C.

267
Tots have wandered over grass both before and after Christ.

268
A lucid stamp of the foot goes well with hoping for the best.

269
The presence of facts in a mind makes for more room for facts.

270
The best should never be liked second best.

271
It was a whole sunbeam.

272
Life, like death, can be a means of stopping mistakes.

273
The personalities of *all* the dead are as vivid as
ever.

274
Presuming that three little chicks didn't go peck-
ing about in the ice age, is somehow useful.

275
The name Florabelle remained on the moss-
covered, weather-beaten gravestone for years and
years.

276
You have just been in contact with the flutter of
a butterfly.

277
Any verb can be used of time.

278
To criticize the ancient world is a privilege
which very few use adequately.

279
We don't know who we are unless we like asking.

280
History should revive past griefs for a happy
purpose.

281
A long blade of grass can be newly anywhere.

282
A lovely trait of man is to be seen in the fact that he made up angels, better than himself.

283
The present is always climax, transition, and omen.

284
Only those who have tried know how hard it is to find something not informative whatsoever.

285
Bitten fingernails give way after a while to un-bitten fingernails, for there is Design in nature.

286
There is just as little true love of books as of people.

287
The first rainfall of the world may be considered as having been successful.

288
Things say So and Not So; and more.

289
The world is a big Thus; and more.

290
Every thing answers the questions What? How? and Why?—and asks the question Why Not?

291
Bright things exist by the thousands.

292
To be witty about the law of the conservation of energy would do nobody any harm.

293
Imagination gives warmth to If, and makes the abstract fact.

294
Eternity is the most faithful thing there is.

295
The unconscious of a person is everything he doesn't know which acts on him, or causes him to act; this unconscious can be seen as *in* him.

296
Until immorality is made dull, it has a future.

297
We take our depths with us wherever we go.

298
Science comes from the knowing that you want to know.

299
The beautiful can fill immense warehouses, but shouldn't.

300
The untrue is waiting to reform.

301
A self looking for justification and not finding it feels horrible.

302
Let us contemplate spearpoints on an ancient field of Asia.

303
An unsure person, when truth makes a point, is too often stabbed, not inspired.

304
When you don't see something in the world, ask for it.

A fat woman takes up time and space.

305
Misbehaving with reality is finding it dull.

306
If the terrible didn't exist, we'd miss it.

307
We are not through with anything.

308
A fat woman takes up time and space.

309
We shall always be able to say: Soon.

310
Nature will never grow tired.

311
A dandelion is a scheme of nature.

312
We should be able to bear liking something tremendously.

313
Ignorance is dreary.

314
Foolishness is not taking advantage of the advantageous.

315
X Cruelty is a certain frequent compound of snob-bishness and pain.

316
X What hurts you, more than likely doesn't have to.

317
X At last we have now.

318
Something has always avoided death.

319
X A fish wants to know more.

320
X The reason you're pleased tomorrow ought to hold up in the next century.

321
X Desire is conquered by being approved.

322
X The known and unknown are bigger than you think.

323
X The unknown is coming 'round the block.

Our hidden selves mean well; but not as hidden.

324
The unexperienced ought not to be permanent.

325
Silence ought to be thrilling, too.

326
Undoubtedly, Perhaps, and No all deserve to win at times, in a person, amid cheers; when one of these is not winning clearly, it should be helping the other two and be helped by them.

327
Our hidden selves mean well; but not as hidden.

328
Bliss is a fact.

329
We can say, Oh! to anything.

330
Yes can be sterner than No on occasion.

331
Maybe and However met and started trouble.

332
When we are what we are, there's nothing to complain about.

333

X   A nervous person has himself in his clutches.

334

X   Our approach to the new can be fresher.

335

The best raptures sing under examination.

336

Grassblades are so strange and so unpretending.

337

Treetops fully understood can help the concept of Christianity.

338

X   A person displeased with himself wants to meet the facts, but not often.

339

X   Peace of mind is paved with honest intentions. ━

340

X   If you're willing to be different, you are different.

341

X   To be intellectual is to be unable not to meet objects; and to be unable to meet objects without giving them order.

342
The rule of ourselves is a subjugation of dullness.

343
X Ants are industrious; so are oceans.

344
X To think is to give blood a chance to do its stuff.

345
X When man tries the most, he is the most satisfied.

346
In so far as the future will have a grassblade in it, it is a grassblade.

347
X Let us immediately be fair to the remote.

348
X A mother can be the best friend of her child, among others.

349
X Right now an auto is coming towards you where a stagecoach might have.

350
X Stars and years have always been faithful to each other.

351

Tell the truth about yourself to yourself, or you'll think you've been deceived and grow angry.

352

When you use the word *Me,* see what the boys in the back room will have.

353

Know that you are something looking for something in a way that means something more.

354

Do whatever you please, but be sure it *is* what you *please.*

355

To know what you want is a lifetime job and should be.

356

Within all conflagrations mathematical things are related.

357

Whenever the roulette wheel of self is turned, someone may get the wrong number.

PART TWO

1

When a self is happy, it is critical of its own happiness in so far as a self is a process, and process implies criticism.

2

When a self is in love, it is in, of, for, and around an object at once; the object is likewise in, of, for, and around it at once.

3

Infinity is a practical matter; it is a way of getting where you want and being in motion at the same time.

4

The first thing necessary in dealing with a conflict in self is to know what it's about, to know what you want to win, and also not to mind winning: this feeling can exist at once in triple shape.

5

We ask questions of ourselves all the time; we won't be happy in the answer if we do not ask the question happily.

6

When we have vanity, or 2-A, we go after less than what we want by regarding it as all that we want.

7

The self is so made that it can watch its watchfulness, like its regret, regret its triumph, and look at its vigilance in remembering; this can give an idea of the interaction of doing and looking, and doing-looking present in the self: the doing-looking is the Aesthetic Realism way of terming the subject-object or object-subject relation.

8

The self can watch itself becoming lazy, or non-watchful; this is an asset that can make both for humor and profound well-being.

9

It is a privilege to let things act on us in keeping with their being; the uncomposed person has changed this privilege into a secret, dull, constant burden.

10

If a person can't love the sun, he can't love a woman.

11

Life can be a proof of the indescribable desirability of being born.

12

Where reality begins, the Why of a thing, or its purpose, is its being, or its thingness; and reality can just as well begin now as a long time ago.

13

If a person is closely logical and likes it, at that moment his body, including his stomach, is fond of syllogisms.

14

Desires have their ups and downs just as kingdoms do, and the history of both can be written.

15

We never disliked a thing in the wrong way without disliking ourselves, too.

16

No one has yet found out all the ways that joy may be had, or all the ways that pain can be seen usefully.

17
The study of the world is a study of pleasure.

18
Love is a way the self has of announcing it has got to something and doesn't mind.

19
As soon as anything is thought of and thought of even to be hated, the self is saying, "Me and my partner."

20
We can know precisely, definitely, rigidly that we imagine freely, soaringly, weirdly.

21
History is made up of feelings over, which, as soon as they are known now, come to life again, for they affect us.

22
If pleasure is not useful, it isn't pleasure.

23
We can become romantic about reality just as it is; in fact, if we are not romantic about reality, we haven't seen it just as it is.

24

Since everyone is in the world, it does seem a little silly, doesn't it, not to know what we're in and what it's about; true philosophy does show that it is silly.

25

We should love South America and a Brazilian girl for the same reason.

26

A person, caring for another, can do nothing more affectionate than making beauty in general more intimate for the loved person; he or she does this because general beauty has been welcomed in the parlor.

27

Every time we think of a person who is dead, that person is a live number.

28

What Alice, a little girl in Elizabethan times, daughter of a tavern keeper in Deptford, found out about Will Shakespeare one summer's afternoon in 1605, while helping her father in the tavern, is now sought for with bibliographical zeal in the colleges of five continents; and the search should go on.

29

Everyday love can change into eternal love, and still be everyday and sensible.

30

If the journey to truth does not have in it the quality of a fierce gallop, and of the steady, lumbering covered wagon, and of a most grand waltz, it isn't truth that is being journeyed towards.

31

Fakers have a motive, but they can't fool themselves into really liking it.

32

There is nothing beautiful in the world disconnected from ourselves and our heartbeat.

33

At any moment of beauty, that moment can spread out, take in more territory, and at the same time behave neatly.

34

Even in death we are not out of the world; the world is forgiving and won't let us.

35

To be living at any moment is such a success, such a triumph that all the pens in history have only scratched the surface.

Man has the rat and the angel in him; this situation can be solved by having wings also dig.

36

When two selfish persons meet, they resent themselves specifically but approve of themselves abstractly, no end.

37

Man has the rat and the angel in him; this situation can be solved by having wings also dig.

38

Everyone should ask: Is that thing I? If the question is wholly asked, the answer will be, Yes.

39

Selfishness, in the bad sense, exists because the deepest basis of the self is not accepted: the deepest things in self, the very deepest, are the best; if we go as deep as might be into the self at any time, we shall reach innocence and knowledge.

40

The self can slink; the self can crawl; the self can cower; but a self can also say it doesn't like it; the fact that a self can criticize what it is, is its resplendent justification.

41

We cannot like anything wholly unless we like the world that goes with it; or otherwise we like it as against the world, and this spiritually doesn't pay.

42

Every person now alive is a culmination of history.

43

If a self is not happy in grand intentions and precise intentions, it has accepted cheapness.

44

Vagueness can be a weapon of the self when it's up to mischief.

45

If people were more interested in being good than in being better, they would be happier.

46

The unconscious is satisfied with incompleteness only when it honestly goes after completeness.

47

There are ups and downs, ins and outs, nears and fars, tos and froms in the self all the while there is one immeasurably quiet point, one immeasurably smooth surface, one perfect circle, one cube, one sphere, and one one.

48

Only a person who loves people can be alone rightly.

49

The purpose of a mother should be the doing away with the need in the child of her as mother; just as the purpose of a doctor should be the doing away with the need of himself as doctor.

50

A person who sees himself as in love with someone and cannot be happy away from that someone is not in love; for the meaning of that someone does not go very far.

51

A mother should be happy when her child can be truly happy away from her.

52

It takes strength to like strength.

53

It is more important to deserve to be loved than apparently to have love.

54

People are unhappy often because they feel they don't deserve to be happy.

55

We can watch our words, our feelings, our fingers, and mist at the same time.

56

The mysterious unconscious can make for definite howling and indefinite yammering.

57

X The unconscious of every person is the whole world.

58

The sun gets under our eyelids, also within our ears.

59

X The word *We* has no limits when you come to think of it; and the word *I* can be like a prairie if you let it.

60

X Being faithful to the unknown is being faithful to ourselves.

61

X If we knew what we needed, it would surprise us.

62

To sit in the sun is sometimes our destiny.

63

X The inevitable is amiable.

To sit in the sun is sometimes our destiny.

64

X Look at what you came from; look at what you're going to, and don't stop.

65

X On every subject the best thing can be said.

66

X Delia has a great advantage in knowing Delia.

67

X Harry is inconsistent on the subject of Harry.

68

A cat captures something of us.

69

X Those who met death at Waterloo are more talked of generally than those who met death elsewhere.

70

X When Delia found out about Dave she looked on lettuce differently.

71

X The inwardly unfortunate person, or as he used to be called, the neurotic, changes many a nice And into a disreputable But.

72

When we grow, we come to be what we are by coming to be what we have not been.

73

The more we desire the more respectable we are; desire is a sign that we appreciate Reality as Deity.

74

Things are appreciative of everything you see of them.

75

A pessimist is a person who wants the half-truth, the half-truth, and nothing but the half-truth.

76

We are of the world; our job is to be fair to the preposition.

77

Of anything we can say: Its reality is our hope.

78

A possibility should be an asset.

79

When she loved Him she also loved Them: Cheers.

Things are appreciative of everything you see of them.

80
X If the world were a girl it would be a nice, brilliant, and progressive girl.

81
Snakes get around, so do pins.

82
When a rose dies, the part which was thorn may change into a petal.

83
X When flattery is useful it is stern injustice.

84
The last hour has been brought to a meaningful conclusion.

85
— X We should respect what we understand and what we don't understand.

86
X Truth is in a quiet rush.

87
Prairies are quiet and efficient.

88
X The Rocky Mountains sweetly await understanding.

89

X The schizophrenic has come to think that it is better to have all of half of himself, than it is to go after all of himself.

90

Among those present in a disturbed person's mind are some exacting dignitaries he does not know.

91

X It is never too late to ask, "Who am I?"

92

X None of us has heard the complete news about ourselves.

93

X What he said to her and what he said to himself disagreed to the advantage of neither.

94

X I and it should be better friends.

95

X We are integrating or disintegrating as we go down the stairs.

96

What we rightly might have done should have charmed us into acquiescence.

97
Have you a little interference in your soul?

98
What the Romans wholly desired was not got.

99
A world that can make rocks and Max Beerbohm is pretty good.

100
We are all somewhat.

101
Only you can be all you.

102
What we avow in our hearts should make us proud as hell.

103
Everyone can say My Pacific Ocean if he knows how.

104
A friend is a person who takes care of himself by being friendly to you.

105
To ourselves we are always being introduced.

106
Me and a stranger are always found in dreams.

107
In the deepest unconscious "with sincerity" means with energy.

108
X The austerity of nature asks that sex really be desired.

109
X Grace is a way of doing something simply and completely and as if you weren't: it is the negation of fuss.

110
X That which we were is present in that which we are; we should know how if we want to take full advantage of that which we are.

111
When the new and old collide, something superfluous has taken place.

112
The Western Hemisphere doesn't mind as such if ring-around-the-rosy is played in it.

113
X Woman is one of the best sexes we have.

114
X The homosexual is bad not so much because he likes his sex but because he is unfair to the other.

115
X We should insist on what we deserve after having insisted on deserving it.

116
X If we get what we don't deserve, we are being misunderstood.

117
A dog's howl is a criticism of a kind.

118
X What is, is with everything it has.

119
X What we don't know may disappoint us.

120
X A just resentment is more beautiful than an unjust approbation.

121
The distinctive should be seen so.

122
X When she spoke to him insincerely, he helped.

123
X Love, as we find it most often, is an arrangement by which two people become less than themselves with apparent comfort and glamour.

124
X Our great moments should be just that.

125
In Cairo he didn't find out something which he didn't know in Wilkes-Barre.

126
The person he adored wasn't she; the person doing the adoring wasn't he: all this is not a reflection on adoration.

127
X What *doesn't* care?

128
What we're used to, if explored, will surprise.

129
X Dynamite is coherent, explosive, and obedient.

Love, as we find it most often, is an arrangement by which two people become less than themselves with apparent comfort and glamour.

130
There is novelty in ethics, and virtue in surprise.

131
X Every self is original if it gets down to it: this may not happen.

132
X Vanity can be brutal and conceit ruthless.

133
There can be slatternly ethics and ill-kept moral sense and untidy religion.

134
The self, in so far as it is courageous, is neat.

135
The unconscious can like briskness, too.

136
Green leaves enter our ears, and logic enters our pores.

137
If a poem isn't good, it isn't much, and it lacks virtues in proportion as it is dull.

138
Murderers want to get ahead, as do sea captains.

139

An overcoat can wrap around our personal history, including our secret history which may never be known, let alone written.

140

X Knowledge, like tomatoes, ought to be joy-giving.

141

X Suffering can be seen beautifully and exactly.

142

X God is the great unconscious looking for representatives and expression.

143

X The bad should be seen with sincere contempt; and the dismal with tingling disdain.

144

X If one could say, "Hooray for poetry!" sincerely, the Hooray would be appropriate and continuously justifiable.

145

There is the logic of the heartbeat; it is always cheerful and is more subtle than pessimism in books and out of them.

146
The moon waited for centuries to have jazz played under it.

147
X One purpose of astronomy is to be fair to the moon; to do away with its conceptual loneliness.

148
The unconscious was prepared to express itself through autumn leaves.

149
X What we can know about dead people has no boundaries.

150
What makes words together right is what makes an orange right.

151
X The seeing of the ugly as ugly is beautiful.

152
X To understand pain is to be pleased.

153
X Tears can cause commotion anywhere.

154
When you say something well, space is helped.

155
The very center of the world is everything.

156
X The decade 1620-1630 has dead people whom we
don't know and who can mean something to us.

157
X He sneezed a couple of thousand times before he
died of drowning.

158
Death settles, unsettles, confuses, and is neg-
lected.

159
The future of Henry VIII is in progress.

160
X So many pains of the past we lack sympathy
with!

161
Mysterious beauty was caused by that which
made the humdrum, the boring, and the so far
unjudged.

162

She came of a good family and didn't see twigs rightly.

163

A sentimental person, in the bad sense, is one who, not truly believing in loveliness, is in too much of a hurry to see it.

164

Both Beryl and Bernard can be soft-headed and hard-hearted.

165

The bishop at Pentecost can talk of divine things like infinity greasily and of the crucifixion oilily.

166

Beauty has a great past, a great present, and more.

167

The whole world can be thought of in the twinkling of an eye, or in the running for a streetcar.

168

Correct desires are always successful, for to have correct desires is to succeed.

169

Let us not be angry at the way we are angry.

170
Whatever the world does, it's secure; nothing can be snugger than existence.

171
We could spend a lifetime counting the dead.

172
Every classic of the past is an instance of death not interfering with possible pleasure.

173
The unconscious goes towards architecture.

174
The unconscious is disappointed at times if we're not disappointed.

175
At any moment of the world, there is a Great Pause.

176
These things are in tears: instruction, content, direction, possibility.

177
Vanity says: This is true because of what I am.

178
In 1846 there was pleasure, in 1847 there was

ϗ pain from the pleasure without the possessor's knowing it; this makes the pleasure worth questioning.

179
ϗ The ego can be a tiger, a city cat, a continent, and a mite.

180
The world is neat.

181
ϗ It takes time to know time.

182
You cannot object to life or find no meaning in it unless you are alive. If the objecting to life is correct, then something good can be done in life. If the objecting is incorrect, then life is good anyway.—If one finds no meaning in life, then the finding is significant or meaningful or not. If the finding is meaningful, then there is meaning in life; if the finding is meaningless, then finding no meaning in life is useless and incorrect.

183
ϗ One of the objects of life is to find useful objections to it.

184
ϗ A rose-petaled ego has a thorny time of it.

185
Infinity, like shoes, should be seen properly.

186
Infinity was around a moment ago.

187
Knowing what all our fears are can be a sumptu-
ous experience.

188
Space can be luscious.

189
A good poem is good for everybody, including
those who never heard of it.

190
What the unconscious most wants to avoid is
what it needs most.

191
A name is now waiting for an unborn child.

192
If we don't live long enough to see our mistakes,
it's a mistake.

193
No day in history is completely known.

A name is now waiting for an unborn child.

194
One should be a logician to his fingertips.

195
The very next thing can be dealt with more beautifully.

196
The day after tomorrow is in our bones.

197
Making the world less than it is, is unfair to ourselves; its magnitude is our well being.

198
The trouble with marriage is that it isn't.

199
Alexander Graves was nobody until he died: this was fortunate and unfortunate.

200
Being oneself is a lifetime job, not to be shirked when we sleep.

201
It's poetic things in the world that make the poet, that make the poem.

202
Fury can be found in unintermittent, logical thought.

203
Every one of us who lived in 1928 went through three minutes on June 14, 1928.

204
In poetry, mind meets world with courage.

205
To accept a less important pleasure as against a more important pleasure is to be against pleasure.

206
Everything in the world wants to be useful.

207
We can take thrilling expeditions under our skin.

208
The unknown is ready.

209
The next moment can be so utterly new.

210
The word *Reality* has an indefinite number of well disposed exclamation marks after it.

Our skeletons make merry when we do.

211
He who likes art and doesn't like life, doesn't know what he's aesthetic about; he who likes life and doesn't like art, doesn't know what he's living for.

212
The world will never stop making demands on you; if it did, it would let you down.

213
The chair had her; he didn't: when the bed had her later, he didn't either.

214
Our skeletons make merry when we do.

215
What does a cute body really mean?

216
In such a time, the time should be such.

217
Expectancy lasts.

218
The fact that a thing was done rightly will never be not a fact.

219

The elegant is eternal; and the frivolous in infinite; and warmth is millions of miles away, too.

220

Beauty may go, but what makes beauty, never.

221

The world can be up to anything; there is mischief in it, attended by form.

222

Seventeen persons can be wrong in fifteen different ways about one thing.

223

A beautiful girl may be as confused as a dammed-up river.

224

A lucid thought can twinkle cheerily.

225

He was dull in a flash.

226

We have a right to an opinion about the year 1980.

227

In 1842 more was found out about 1524.

228
Brooks ran merrily in imperial Rome.

229
Our unconscious can be fickle about the moon.

230
The more we see things, the more we can be passionate gracefully.

231
Vanity can take the sculptured form of reason.

232
He feared the on-coming of pimples and death, at the same time.

233
Lora had her way with Ted and got an earache two hours later, which may have had nothing to do with Ted.

234
A pimple has atoms to it; and mucus has electrons.

235
When we're alive, we have survived everything.

236
Thomas Shadwell, seventeenth-century drama-

tist, took up the professor's time, as did Shadwell's wife.

237
The time of all orgasms taken together may fill centuries.

238
The ecstasies of the past should never be forgot.

239
We should make the world measure up to our good times and surpass them.

240
God is an infinite good time.

241
God is evolution considered personally.

242
Incompleteness should make one indignant.

243
Evolution helps us dress well.

244
If anything matters, truth matters, because without it we can't know anything matters.

245
Years, years, and years ago people were told to shut up; and to a degree, rightly.

246
A self is an object that can know what it is, and therefore the largeness of the self depends on the largeness of the knowledge which the self has of what it is.

247
One cannot like a thing which one does not know, and therefore if a self does not know what it is, it cannot like what it is; what the self may like when it does not know what it is, is not the whole self.

248
Knowing an object is having a state of mind adequate to what that object is: here an inner situation is the equivalent of an outer situation and is just to it.

249
We cannot be fair to a person or any other thing without knowing it: knowing is justice here.

250
Loving something is either just or unjust; if it is not just it is not love; it is either flattery or pity.

251
At any one moment the mind is dealing with an object. An object needs a self in order to be known.

252
In any instance of knowing, the self becomes more.

253
Any object met becomes forever part of the self which meets it.

254
A self can meet other selves to its growth or to its lessening.

255
The only way a self grows is by knowing; therefore if in love, a self is desiring something else than knowing, it is desiring its lessening.

256
Experience is what remains in a self after meeting an object.

257
A self either welcomes or dismisses experience; if it welcomes experience, in proportion that it does, it wishes to organize it.

258
The organization of anything is the finding or making of unity while diversity is welcomed.

259
We love an object in so far as through it we can find a means of organization of what we are.

260
All organization is aesthetic in so far as aesthetics is a situation of manyness and sameness, or manyness as sameness.

261
A self is happy while it can welcome objects in such a way as to find out the oneness of what it is.

262
All happiness of a self is aesthetics.

263
A self essentially is a certain way of affirming its own existence by affirming the existence of existence.

264
When we love, we are; for love is the sensational, accurate acceptance of an object as a means of our own being.

265
We know through our bodies, too.

266
We know all the time, but we do not wholly know unless we know the object we are knowing singly and as related to other objects.

267
When a thing is related to another, it has something in common with that thing; all things have something in common with each other.

268
Pleasure is the deep acceptance of a relation, commonness, or oneness with something; pain is the rejection of such relation, commonness, or oneness.

269
Our bodies know; every organ in our bodies knows; whatever our bodies do has body-knowledge with it.

270
We do not participate in any action completely unless we know that action; for to know, in the full sense, is to experience.

When a thing is related to another, it has something in common with that thing; all things have something in common with each other.

271
The rejection of knowing is the welcoming of death.

272
Whenever a self exists, it is the world as that self.

273
Insanity is the disruption of the idea of the self as world and the world as self, existing simultaneously.

274
To be nervous is to be unready, unwilling, or unable to welcome the full existence of oneself.

275
The self is an aesthetic proposition.

276
The self is always criticizing what it is.

277
The self is a relation of particularity and generality shown through a body.

278
Criticism in a self is that which drives it to its

completeness; criticism blurred or unwelcomed makes for lessening and death.

279
Every element or constituent of a self is looking for relation, width, or organization with every other element of a self and with everything else: all at the same time.

280
Every aspect of body is how the self takes form or behaves.

281
In so far as a self comes from the world, a knowledge of the world is in it; it is a self because it can come to be aware, wants to be aware of that knowledge of the world in it.

282
Sex is a symbolical way of accepting an object by saying that one is of the object while the object is of one; that one is in the object while the object is in one.

283
The unconscious in a self, that is, that in a self it does not see and therefore does not completely have, is aesthetic when seen.

284
Aesthetics is a situation seen as having difference as sameness, sameness as difference. Rest and motion, oneness and manyness, structure and function, form and substance, line and color, intellect and emotion are all phases of the sameness and difference situation.

285
The I wants to be complete by seeing what it is as actually, concretely, immediately, always, generally different from everything else and the same as everything else.

286
When we see a dish, what the unconscious feels is that we are the same as the dish and different from the dish at once; this goes for all perception.

287
All perception completely had is aesthetic, that is, the perceiver, in complete perception, will have a sense of the difference between it and the thing perceived, and the sameness with it, and a set of in between combinations of sameness and difference: that is, the self here will feel its uniqueness, its aloneness; its being of all things, its comprehensiveness; and it will also feel, having an awareness of absoluteness, that it is imperfect, *something,* in process.

288
A sense of perfection and a sense of process at once is in the aesthetic situation.

289
One loves a thing in proportion to how much the love of this thing makes one at ease with other things.

290
If good exists and we don't know it, we are robbed.

291
Planets have not yet said they believe in pretending.

292
One tear can hit another tear in the exact center.

293
If a person isn't proud to love someone, he might as well begin over again with apologies to himself.

294
People rarely talk about *themselves.*

295
Conceit can moan, bellow, stutter, yawn, and do nothing at all.

Conceit can moan, bellow, stutter, yawn, and do nothing at all.

296
It hasn't yet been scientifically proved that any lovely thing is really over.

297
People should meet and people should leave each other in order to improve themselves.

298
People who don't know why they love, should.

299
The good thing that happened yesterday was needed long ago.

300
If we do right, whether we know it or not, like it or not, we imitate others who have done right.

301
The right thing is always original.

302
Deeply we fear getting what we don't deserve; getting what we don't deserve sorely embarrasses the unconscious.

303
Considering how much is being felt in the world should stagger one into an easy, lilting ecstasy.

304
Yes, but the repository of the furies, longings, surprises, victorious passions of the past *is* the large library.

305
When anything at all happens, it happens plumply and squarely in the universe.

306
Excitement should be steady.

307
There are three kinds of men: dead men, living men, and unborn men; these three kinds of men meet constantly.

308
If a bellyache persists for just a little longer, the universe can be seen as coming to an end.

309
Henry Watts's mother bore him to be slapped on the face by a girl he didn't know, two decades later.

310
In so far as lust has form, it is commendable; in so far as it does not have form, it is not completely lust.

To be naked under the stars with a good book is unfair neither to yourself, to stars, nor to literature.

311
It is quite correct to praise God if a feminine person smiles rightly.

312
Girls with rosebud lips can be brutal: this should not surprise excessively, nor should one refrain from seeking an explanation.

313
So many girls are sleeping alone tonight, you couldn't count them even if you knew where they were: they are a great anonymous aggregate in current destiny.

314
Beauty should be beautiful in the same way as fire is fiery.

315
To be naked under the stars with a good book is unfair neither to yourself, to stars, nor to literature.

316
Biological laws, seen subtly, can make a girl proud.

317
If a person twiddles his finger, his organic judg-

ment thinks it best to do so: there is choice behind a twitch, and stark inevitability in a tic.

318
Stern truth becomes sweeter the more you know of it.

319
If a dumb girl is beautiful, there is some opposition to dumbness.

320
It was a joyous three-quarters of an hour, consisting of three definitely pleasant fifteen minute periods.

321
We should speak of God with affection and esteem, avoiding gush wherever possible; rapture, however, need not be discountenanced.

322
Her cough was an anthology of her worries.

323
Sometimes he was more hard-hearted than he was confused; sometimes the contrary occurred.

324
Anticipation is one thing; animal training is another.

325
Among all his contemporaries, it was Dorothy he had on his knee.

326
During the Civil War, certain fish were never caught.

327
One can read books in drug stores twice.

328
We should be so bubblingly happy to be surrounded by nothing less than everything.

329
When we're very happy, we do exactly what the world is telling us to do; and we feel, quite rightly, it's what we're telling ourselves to do.

330
Vanity, or wrong self-approval, is a fast horse, but the wrong one.

331
If the trip towards truth isn't pleasant, it isn't the fault of the destination.

332
People who mind each other's business are asking for a second chance.

333
When criticism begins at home, it's in a hurry to leave.

334
To see ourselves as dead ought to be useful for what we do next.

335
To seek, to find, and to seek more meaning in what we find is good sense.

336
Each self is ancient history, current history, and prophecy.

337
If a passionate, beautiful woman enters a grocery, her passion is looking around, too.

338
When one loves, the facts *have* to catch up.

339
To know what you don't want to do is the best way of not doing it; to know what you want to do is the best way of doing it.

340
When you know what you want to do it glitters

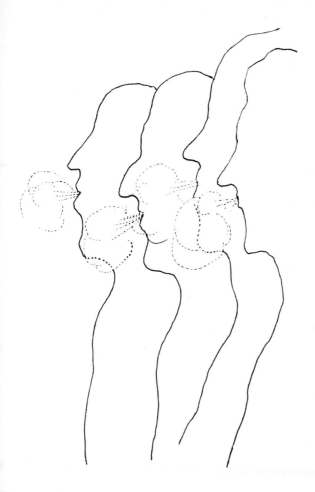

Noses go north as well as breath.

as against what you don't want to do; what you
want to do at this time just lures you on.

341
Every century can be used for our pleasure.

342
No past moment in history is inactive.

343
If a happy person has died, his happiness is true
today.

344
The solar system is man's comrade.

345
Noses go north as well as breath.

346
In understanding grief, we oppose it; in understanding pleasure, we increase it.

347
Electrons are eaten each day.

348
The usefulness of beauty cannot be denied; it is
also hazardous to deny the good looks of the
useful.

349
Music tells sound how to behave.

350
Considering the nature of everything, everything has its place.

351
If anything can please you, don't narrow the field.

352
What never has happened can never have said of it: It can't happen.

353
The best part of animals and plants is also the best part of humans.

354
When we're proud of our feelings, we look on them just as they are.

355
Enough thistledown weighs more than Samuel Johnson.

356
A single stupidity is a common calamity.

357
Only people who know what their selves are, don't have to hide them.

358
We should, with zest, try to understand our sorrow.

359
We can think of mausoleums in the quiet depths of the sea while running fast.

360
When truth is divided, errors multiply.

361
Old fires have not gone out.

362
Things that were are.

363
Letty West owes her pretty nose to Something or Other.

364
If we make the world less, it is we who are meek.

365
The absolute is that which has to exist, whatever else does.

366
The fingers of a vain person are interfered with.

367
Let us contemplate peacefully all future irritations.

368
The absolute is insistent.

369
The electron is well-intentioned.

370
Psychoanalysis frightens more than it convinces; if it convinced more, it would frighten less.

371
Every moment should have its moment's worth.

372
Escape is bad where it is an escape from joy.

373
Soup, used rightly by a mathematician, helps him do better.

374
A layer cake is geometry and layer cake.

The strange really has a smile on its face; you should welcome it with open arms.

375
In poetry, feelings grow into objects and music.

376
In reading well, we let print get under our skin and do wonders.

377
Every moment proves something.

378
Art can make the old surprising, and the new and sudden soothing.

379
The strange really has a smile on its face; you should welcome it with open arms.

380
What in the world but reality could make ecstasy?

381
Soufflé comes from elemental matter.

382
The whole world is behind the idea that the word *carriage* means something which may be drawn by a horse.

383
Marriage is something less than a word.

384
When we grow weary of something we should not grow weary about, we can become excited about the dull.

385
Every Might Have Been is next door to Can Be and eager, how eager, to change to Is.

386
Money is a way of getting a phase of another person's life.

387
Facts are always whispering, uttering, and shouting advice.

388
We can yell into a cube.

389
Joy is a wonderful compound of necessity and welcoming; pleasure, after all, shouldn't be unnecessary.

390
The world is a great wish-granting mechanism.

391
A precise hope is a determination.

392
The sun won't shine tomorrow for no good reason.

393
We can paint meat, eat it, or both.

394
Keep your fingers crossed if you have nothing better to do with them.

395
Nothing can take the place of time, or time is nothing, too.

396
Space won't keep still, and it won't budge either: so give up trying.

397
Space is anybody's friend.

398
In a second, we can mention two centuries.

399
We can jump down three steps, looking at the evening star.

400
Without grocery stores, stars wouldn't have enough to shine on.

401
When Tom Williams had money and a good time, it was more than Tom Williams' money and time which was concerned.

402
The loneliest thing in the world is a comma looking for a sentence.

403
The idea of a grain of sand in an iceberg approaches the idea of loneliness as such.

404
Wheels don't have to go round.

405
If autumn leaves didn't fall, it would be worse.

406
Miss Desire and Miss Necessity are sisters who have been separated since childhood.

407
How we do a thing is part of what we do.

408
Be sure that what you oppose opposes you.

409
Our interest in the Assyrian Empire should be quite personal.

410
That part of ourselves we don't want to know becomes angry.

411
Every This was a That once.

412
Growth is unfortunately avoidable; the need for growth, never.

413
Any desire of ours should be able to do a solo performance in the Yankee Stadium with the bleachers filled.

414
Criticism can be a bluebird.

415
Every flutter of a hummingbird means something.

416
The insect has a Goal; and the amoeba an Aim.

417
The right thing is entirely insistent.

418
The facts never give up.

419
If truth is not invited as a guest, it becomes a porch-climber in the night.

420
Some tears are better than others.

421
The past has just now caught up with us.

422
No moment is really neutral.

423
The future has commendable intentions.

424
Let us think of just a *few* blood cells for a while.

425
The neurotic has an illicit relation with objects, punctuated by neglect.

426

If you look for variety in the world, you will find it; if you look for soothingness, you will find it; so what are you looking for?

427

Without precipitation and the sun, there would be no parasols.

428

The world *does* care.

429

If you watch it, the universe will grin respectfully.

430

Who has measured the delightful?

431

If you presume rightly, you will love your presumption.

432

An idea is an eddy, an island of the mind, connected with a vast mainland.

433

Say Anyhow: aren't you sure you mean it?

434

There are trends in the stomach.

435
The dead man said: This is where I came in.

436
A critic makes a good thing look good.

437
His life was more *his* than life.

438
We can say My Infinity, because without ourselves, we wouldn't know anything about infinity;
but it is also true that without infinity, we
wouldn't be around to say, know, or not know
anything about infinity: all this goes to show
that it is right to say both My Infinity and
Infinity's Me.

439
The decade 1890-1899 in England—so literary,
so ninetyish—had some smiles appreciably more
sincere than others.

440
What may be, in so far as it is thought of, is.

441
Intellect largely consists of finding what you
have in yourself and having what you find elsewhere.

442
It did not happen and we happen to know it.

443
Not is an unseen flower in the garden of time.

444
What the Babylonians possessed they may have lost, but we haven't lost the Babylonians.

445
History should make time more delightful than ever.